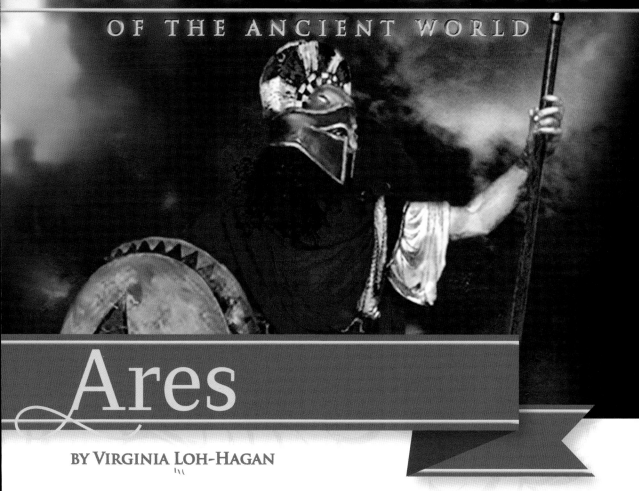

Ares

BY VIRGINIA LOH-HAGAN

Gods and goddesses were the main characters of myths. Myths are traditional stories from ancient cultures. Storytellers answered questions about the world by creating exciting explanations. People thought myths were true. Myths explained the unexplainable. They helped people make sense of human behavior and nature. Today, we use science to explain the world. But people still love myths. Myths may not be literally true. But they have meaning. They tell us something about our history and culture.

45th Parallel Press

Published in the United States of America by Cherry Lake Publishing
Ann Arbor, Michigan
www.cherrylakepublishing.com

Content Adviser: Matthew Wellenbach, Catholic Memorial School, West Roxbury, MA
Reading Adviser: Marla Conn MS, Ed., Literacy specialist, Read-Ability, Inc.
Book Designer: Jen Wahi

Photo Credits: © Igor Zh./Shutterstock.com, 5; © stoyanh/shutterstock.com, 6; © Howard David Johnson, 2016, 8; © Miroslav Trifonov/Shutterstock.com, 11; © Esteban De Armas/Shutterstock.com, 13; © Shotshop GmbH/Alamy Stock Photo, 15; © World History Archive/Alamy Stock Photo, 17; © Mikhail Khromov/istockphoto.com, 19; © Fotokvadrat/Shutterstock.com, 21; © duncan1890/istockphoto.com, 23; © Ezume Images/Shutterstock.com, 24; © Dm_Cherry/Shutterstock.com, 27; © Emma manners/Shutterstock.com, 29; © Howard David Johnson, 2016, Cover; various art elements throughout, shutterstock.com

45th Parallel Press is an imprint of Cherry Lake Publishing.

Library of Congress Cataloging-in-Publication Data

Names: Loh-Hagan, Virginia, author.
Title: Ares / by Virginia Loh-Hagan.
Description: Ann Arbor : Cherry Lake Publishing, [2017] | Series: Gods and goddesses of the ancient world | Includes bibliographical references and index.
Identifiers: LCCN 2016031178| ISBN 9781634721349 (hardcover) | ISBN 9781634722667 (pbk.) | ISBN 9781634722001 (pdf) | ISBN 9781634723329 (ebook)
Subjects: LCSH: Gods, Greek--Juvenile literature. | Mythology, Greek--Juvenile literature.
Classification: LCC BL820.M2 L64 2017 | DDC 292.2/113--dc23
LC record available at https://lccn.loc.gov/2016031178

Printed in the United States of America
Corporate Graphics

ABOUT THE AUTHOR:

Dr. Virginia Loh-Hagan is an author, university professor, former classroom teacher, and curriculum designer. She thinks her dogs are descendants of Ares. They go into a battle frenzy when the doorbell rings. She lives in San Diego with her very tall husband and very naughty dogs. To learn more about her, visit www.virginialoh.com.

TABLE OF CONTENTS

CHAPTER 1

GOD OF WAR

Who is Ares? Who kidnapped him? Who raised him?

Ares was a Greek god. He's the god of war. He's one of the 12 **Olympians**. These gods were the rulers of the gods. They lived on Mount Olympus. Mount Olympus is in Greece. It's the highest mountain in Greece.

Ares is the son of Zeus and Hera. Zeus was the king of the gods. Hera was the queen of the gods. They didn't like Ares. They didn't help when Ares got kidnapped.

Giants wanted to fight Olympians. They wanted to win. So, they took Ares. They locked him in a bronze jar.

Ares was trapped for 13 months. He started losing his mind. The giants' stepmother found out. She told Hermes. Hermes was the gods' messenger. He released Ares.

Hera sent Ares to Priapus. Priapus was a **minor** god. Minor gods aren't as important as major gods. He was a god of male body parts. He raised Ares. He trained Ares.

Ares's father, Zeus, was the god of the sky.

Ares was born and raised in Thrace.

He taught him dancing. He taught him sports. He taught him **martial arts**. Martial arts are fighting skills.

Hera paid Priapus for his service. She said he could take part of Ares's war **spoils**. Spoils are stolen goods. So, Priapus made sure Ares was a good fighter.

Ares never married. He had many lovers. He had many children with different women.

His greatest love was Aphrodite. Aphrodite was the goddess of love. She was his half-sister. But that didn't matter.

Family Tree

Grandparents: Cronus (god of time) and Rhea (goddess of fertility)

Parents: Zeus (god of the sky), Hera (goddess of women and marriage)

Brother: Hephaestus (god of fire and craftsmen)

Sisters: Eileithyia (goddess of childbirth), Enyo (goddess of war), Eris (goddess of strife), Hebe (goddess of youth)

Lover: Aphrodite (goddess of love)

Children with Aphrodite: Phobos (god of fear), Deimos (god of terror), Harmonia (goddess of harmony), Eros (god of love), Anteros (god of requited love), Himeros (god of desire), Pothos (god of longing)

Aphrodite was beautiful. She inspired love. They had an affair. They had several children.

But Aphrodite was married to Hephaestus. He was Ares's brother. Hephaestus was the god of fire and craftsmen. He found out about their affair. He was mad. He trapped them in a net. Ares and Aphrodite were naked. Hephaestus called the other gods. The gods watched them. They made fun of them. Ares felt ashamed. He left Olympus.

 Ares was handsome. He was brave.

CHAPTER 2

WARRIOR

What's the difference between Athena and Ares? How was Ares helpful?

Ares had a sad childhood. His parents didn't love him. But Ares loved his father. Ares killed Ekhidnades for Zeus. Ekhidnades was Zeus's enemy. He was a giant. His feet were snakes. He fought against Zeus. Ares killed him.

Athena was Ares's half-sister. She was the goddess of wisdom and war. Zeus loved Athena very much. This upset Ares.

Ares loved war. He loved violence. He was brutal. He didn't care who won. He just loved the fighting. Athena was different. She fought for good causes. She planned war. She focused on war strategies.

Not many gods liked Ares. They thought he was dangerous. But Hades liked him. Hades was his uncle. He was the god of the underworld. Hades collected dead souls. Ares killed people in war. He brought Hades their souls.

Ares was the most hated god on Mount Olympus.

All in the Family

Hippolyta was Ares's daughter. Her mother was an Amazon. Hippolyta became queen of the Amazons. Amazons were female warriors. They descended from Ares. They only raised girls. They killed male babies. Ares gave Hippolyta his magical girdle. A girdle is a belt. It holds swords. Heracles was a Greek hero. He was given a challenge. He had to get Hippolyta's girdle. Hippolyta fell in love with Heracles. She would've given Heracles the belt. But Hera spread a rumor. She told everyone that Heracles was planning on kidnapping Hippolyta. So, the Amazons attacked Heracles's ships. Heracles felt betrayed. He killed Hippolyta. He took her belt. He sailed away.

Ares was the god of courage.

Sisyphus was a king. He tricked people. He shared the gods' secrets. He kidnapped Thanatos. Thanatos was the god of death. Sisyphus chained Thanatos. That meant no one could die. This made Hades mad. This made Ares mad. No one could die in war.

Ares freed Thanatos. He captured Sisyphus. He brought him to Hades. This showed Ares's loyalty. He helped his uncle. He wanted his uncle to have justice.

In one version of the story, Hades punished Sisyphus. Sisyphus had to roll a big rock uphill. Hades made the rock roll back down. Sisyphus rolled the rock back up. He did this forever.

Ares caused riots. He caused rebellions. But he also created **civil** order. Civil means related to citizens. He brought things back to normal. Then, he upset things. He kept himself busy.

 Ares represented bold force and strength.

CHAPTER 3

BLOODTHIRSTY

Why was Ares unpopular? How did the gods shame him? How and why did he seek revenge?

Mortals and gods needed Ares in battle. Mortals are humans. Ares's fighting style was crazy. He believed in direct combat. He attacked. He destroyed. He fought for blood. This made him useful. This made him a good warrior. But he was also unpopular. He got mad easily. He was aggressive. He wasn't fun. This made him a bad friend.

The gods liked to shame him. They made mortals doubt Ares's power. Ares lost many battles. He couldn't win against Athena. Athena had Zeus's support. Once, Athena hit him with a rock. She knocked him out.

During the Trojan War, Ares fought on the losing side. Athena fought on the winning side. Diomedes was a Greek hero. He drove a spear into Ares's side. Athena helped him. Ares fled to Mount Olympus. He was in pain. Zeus yelled at Ares. But he healed Ares.

Ares represented the bloody side of battle.

Real World Connection

The United States has the world's strongest military. Navy SEALs are the best of the best. They're warriors. They're super soldiers. They're like Ares and Athena combined. They have Ares's war strength. They have Athena's war wisdom. SEAL stands for Sea, Air, and Land. SEALs are a special operations force. They can fight in the sea. They can fight in the air. They can fight on land. They can fight in any environment. They're well-trained. They have special skills. They do top-secret missions. They do dangerous missions. They help win wars. They protect people. They bring peace.

Ares was called a "curse on men."

Ares sought **revenge**. Revenge is getting even. In one story, Ares got jealous. Aphrodite fell in love with Adonis. Adonis was the god of beauty and desire. Ares changed into a boar. Adonis went hunting. Ares tore Adonis apart. He killed Adonis.

Ares's love affair with Aphrodite was hard. They had to sneak around. They hid from Hephaestus. Ares asked Alectryon to stand guard. Alectryon was supposed to warn Ares of spies. Helios was the god of the sun. He caught Ares and Aphrodite together. He told Hephaestus. Ares lost Aphrodite. He blamed Alectryon.

Ares was mad. He turned Alectryon into a rooster. Alectryon had to watch the sun. He cried out. He announced the sun rising. He did this every day. He never forgot to do it. He learned his lesson.

 Ares had swift feet. He was fast.

CHAPTER 4

DEATH TOOLS

What are Ares's weapons? What are his symbols?

Ares had many weapons. His weapons had blood stains. He had a sword. He had a spear. He had a shield. He had a flaming torch. His most special weapon was his helmet. He either wore or held his helmet. He always had it with him.

He rode his war **chariot** everywhere. A chariot is a cart. It has two wheels. It was pulled by four horses. They breathed fire. They were named Fire, Clashing, Flame, and Terror. He also had a throne. His throne was covered with human skin.

Ares went to battlefields with his sisters. They fought together. His sisters were Eris and Enyo. They were

Ares brought death and terror to everyone.

Ares's birds are also called Arean Birds.

goddesses of strife and war. Like Ares, they caused trouble.

Ares had many soldiers. The soldiers were demons. Kydoimos brought confusion. Makhai represented battles. Hysmina represented combat. Phonos represented **manslaughter**. Manslaughter is unplanned killing. Polemos was the spirit of war. Alala sounded the war cry.

Ares brought vultures. Vultures went to Ares's battlefields.

They ate dead bodies. Ares also had monster birds. The birds were called Ornithes Areos. Their bodies shot out arrows. They guarded Ares's temple.

Cross-Cultural Connection

Oro was the war god of Tahiti. Tahiti is an island in the South Pacific. Oro liked fighting. He was a killer of men. He protected princes. Tahitians **sacrificed** pigs and humans to him. Sacrifices are lives that are given up to honor gods. Oro became the god of peace during peacetime. His peace name was Oro-i-Te-Tea-Moe. This means "Oro of the Spear Laid Down." Oro was the son of creator gods. He wanted a wife. He created a rainbow between the earth and heavens. He traveled across the rainbow. He dressed like a warrior. He wore red. He met Vairumati. Vairumati was a mortal. She was the daughter of the first man. They got married. They had a son. Their son became a great ruler. Oro flew across the sky. He changed into a flame. He made Vairumati into a goddess.

CHAPTER 5

FATHER OF A DRAGON

How did Ares help found Thebes?

There are many myths about Ares. Ares helped found a city. The city is Thebes.

The Ismenian Dragon was one of Ares's children. It was a giant monster. It guarded a sacred spring. Cadmus was a Greek hero. He killed the dragon. Ares told Cadmus to pull out the dragon's teeth. Cadmus planted the teeth. The teeth grew into soldiers.

Ares threw stones at the soldiers. The soldiers fought each other. They didn't know who was attacking them. They killed each other. Only five soldiers lived. They became the first Thebans.

Ares was mad about his son's death. He turned Cadmus into his slave. Cadmus served Ares for 8 years. He served his time. Then Ares let Cadmus marry his daughter. Cadmus married Harmonia. All the gods came to their wedding.

The Ismenian Dragon and Ares were both ferocious warriors.

They had babies. This created more people for Thebes. Harmonia brought harmony. Thebes became a peaceful city.

Explained By Science

Ares loved brutal violence. He was aggressive. Charles Darwin believed male aggression was part of survival of the fittest. Men had to be big. They had to be strong. They had to fight off other men. Men like fighting sports. Men like physical jobs. Men have testosterone. Testosterone is a hormone. It makes men more aggressive. Male bodies are built to fight. They have broad shoulders. Men have upper body strength. They're tall. They have more muscles than fat. They have thick jaws. This allows for more punching and throwing. This allows them to use weapons. This allows them to take hits more. Darwin believed these characteristics are leftover from when size and aggression helped men survive.

Gods could hold grudges against each other for a long time.

Ares was still mad. He changed Harmonia and Cadmus into snakes. But the snakes escaped and lived in peace

Don't anger the gods. Ares had great powers. And he knew how to use them.

- Ares was celebrated in Sparta. Sparta was a city in ancient Greece. It was a city of warriors. Spartans made human sacrifices to him. They gave up human lives to honor Ares.

- Enyalios served Ares. He was a minor god of war. Young Spartans sacrificed puppies to him. They did this at night.

- Ares's temples were built outside of cities. They stopped enemies from coming into cities.

- Eros was a child of Ares and Aphrodite. He's more commonly known as Cupid. He had a bow and arrows. He shot at the hearts of mortals and gods. He made them fall in love. He played with their emotions.

- Cycnus was one of Ares's sons. He was evil. He killed travelers. He used their skulls and bones to build temples. Heracles killed him. Ares wanted to get even. He almost killed Heracles. Zeus stepped in. He threw a thunderbolt between Ares and Heracles.

- Ancient Romans worshipped gods. Mars was the Roman version of Ares. Mars was more respected than Ares.

CONSIDER THIS!

TAKE A POSITION Ares loved war for its own sake. He liked battles. He liked killing. But he also protected cities. He protected his family. Was Ares good or evil? Argue your point with reasons and evidence.

SAY WHAT? Ares liked war combat. He directly fought in wars. Athena fought war from a distance. She studied war strategies. Read the 45th Parallel Press book about Athena. Explain how Athena and Ares were the same. Explain how they were different.

THINK ABOUT IT! Waging war is a team effort. Athena provided war wisdom. Ares provided war strength. Eris called forth war. Zeus directed war's outcome. Read the other 45th Parallel Press books about the gods and goddesses. How were the gods and goddesses connected? How did they work together toward a common goal?

LEARN MORE

O'Connor, George. *Ares: Bringer of War.* New York: First Second Books, 2015.

Temple, Teri, and Robert Squier (illustrator). *Ares: God of War.* Mankato, MN: Child's World, 2012.

GLOSSARY

chariot (CHAR-ee-uht) two-wheeled cart pulled by animals

civil (SIV-uhl) related to citizens

manslaughter (MAN-slaw-tur) unplanned killing

martial arts (MAHR-shuhl AHRTS) fighting skills

minor (MYE-nur) secondary

mortals (MOR-tuhlz) humans

Olympians (uh-LIM-pee-uhnz) rulers of the gods who live on Mount Olympus

revenge (rih-VENJ) to get even

sacrificed (SAK-ruh-fise-duh) lives offered to honor gods

spoils (SPOILZ) stolen goods

INDEX